Offerings

A BOOK OF POETRY

BY *Rose of Sharon*

Offerings, A Book of Poetry

Copyright © 2021 by Rose of Sharon

ISBN 978-1-7368204-2-1

Design by Irma Burns with Tell Your Tale Marketing
Photography by Elizabeth Balsam
Rose of Sharon graphic logo by Kristopher Rojas

*I*n honor of the Holy Spirit,
who graciously inspires.

*W*ith gratitude to Jeanne Curcio, Eddie Scales,
Lisa Kimble, and my loving husband Daniel Joseph.
This book would not have been possible
without their support.

*T*hese poems are humble offerings that
I give to God in thanksgiving for the many gifts
he has given me. I also present them as offerings of
hope, peace, and joy to others who are on the journey.

Contents

I. Dawning

II. Trusting

III. *Rejoicing*

IV. *Abiding*

I.

Dawning

Dance the Day

Love
danced the day
you were born.
Love
swaddled your soul,
waltzed around,
and promenaded across the sky.

Love
danced the day
you were born.
Love
started your existence,
continues your journey
and carries you to eternity.

Love
danced the day
you were born.
Love
longs for and desires to see
fullness in your veins
and freedom in your toes.

Love
danced the day
you were born.
I want to dance the day
with Love
and you.

This is the Morn

This is the morn
when darkness was annihilated
by the Son who will never set.

This is the morn
when an empty tomb
proclaimed eternal life.

This is the morn
when mournful Mary
became a joyful witness.

This is the morn
when defeated disciples
ran triumphantly.

This is the morn
when the enslaved were unchained
with the bells of freedom.

This is the morn.
The dawn that was made
for you and me.
Amen! Alleluia!

07.20.1969 Welcome

> "Honor, greetings and blessings to you,
> conquerors of the moon.
> Pale lamp of our nights and our dreams."
>
> Pope Paul VI, July 1969

Honor, greetings and blessings to you,
high respect, great esteem.
Best wishes and goodwill,
divine favor, celestial dream

to you, conquerors of the moon.
Collin, Aldrin, Armstrong;
     Mike, Buzz, and Neil.
Space seekers, summit reachers.
Lunar landing, serenely surreal.

The moon, pale lamp of our nights:
Calendar inspiration, force of tidal sea,
lightly illuminate, faintly reflect,
our eventide, then dark apogee.

Of our nights and our dreams:
Mankind's twilight, aspiration peers to blue.
And her peaceful presence glowingly concurs,
honor, greetings, and blessings to you.

Note: As the 50th anniversary of man's first landing on the moon approached in 2019, the moon attracted my attention more than normal. This poem blossomed out of both the moon's allure and Pope Paul VI's greeting to the astronauts.

Thou

Thou hearest me
    the yawning of my mouth
    the laughter when I play
    the slander that I spread
    and the words I try to pray

Thou seest me
    the hair so sterling sparse
    the scars upon my knees
    the selfish acts I commit
    and when I strive to please

Thou art within me
    the breath that fills my lungs
    the blood that fills my veins
    my heart so full of joy
    and my soul in grieving pain

Thou art everywhere!

Note: Select lines from "Thou" comes from the "Prayer Before Personal Meditation" published in a book of *Prayers* by Miles Christi (https://www.mileschristi.org/) a Religious Order of the Roman Catholic Church.

A Sacred Space

There is a sacred space,
so nurturing and warm.
There is a sacred space,
where **breath** gave you your form.

Within this sacred space,
your heart beat strong and true.
Within this sacred space,
you ate, and swam, and grew.

Within this sacred space,
you felt, and listened, and learned.
Within this sacred space,
you played, and tossed, and turned.

There is a sacred space,
just like your own cocoon.
This sacred space of course,
is called your mother's womb.

She Prayed

Each time she heard the sirens
cutting through the peaceful living
of her youth, she prayed.

She didn't pray
for the safety of the fighters
who handled axes and hoses
and shielded their grey matter with red helmets.

She didn't pray
for all who were subject to the thirsty inferno
that ravenously consumes all it can,
or the dwellings that were in danger
of being incinerated.

No, she prayed for something else.

In the springtime of her existence
and the naïveté of her truth,
her thoughts reached a grim conclusion:
The shrilling sirens, the thunderous trucks,
and the pulsating lights, meant danger!
And the tough men that came –
why, they came to set the fires!

Her simple prayer which she echoed
over and over again, with tightly woven fingers
and pleading lips was this.
"Oh, please don't come to our house,
Oh, please don't come,
Oh, please . . ."

Note: When my mother was a young child, she was terrified of firefighters and firetrucks.
She thought they came to start fires! Her main concern was that they never come to her home.

Crisp Winter Morn

I love swirls of steam
from a mug of warm brew
on a crisp winter morn.

I love sun-lit threads
holding a house of web
on a crisp winter morn.

I love breathing fresh
piercing chilly air
on a crisp winter morn.

I love red berries
feeding cold hungry birds
on a crisp winter morn.

I love dormant trees
with the marrow of spring
on a crisp winter morn.

I love the silent presence
of our peaceful God
on a crisp winter morn.

The Artist at Work

A framing of oceans
A construction of mountains
The Artist at work

A sculpting of glaciers
A welding of cliffs
The Artist at work

A smearing of deserts
A cutting of valleys
The Artist at work

A slicing of rivers
A gluing of canyons
The Artist at work

A stroke of trees
A splash of meadows
The Artist at work

A blending of sun
A shading of clouds
The Artist at work

A spraying of moonbeams
A polishing of stars
The Artist at work

A forming of fish
A shaping of beasts
The Artist at work

The molding of man,
And the breath of life,
Ahhhhhhhh . . .
The Artist's **greatest** work!

II.

Trusting

The Divine Hand Plants

The Divine Hand plants.

He watches two seeds
root and intertwine,
and beams as they
break forth together
from the good earth,
their stems fused
as one.

The Divine Son shines.

The Master Gardener
sends showers,
and the united plant
bears fruit
under the glowing grin
of its Creator.

The Divine Breath blows,

and the plant submits
to the Holy Forces,
allowing the seeds of its fruit
to be stripped
and thrown
into sacred space.

The Divine Hand plants . . .

Dreams

She never had real labor pains
but sometimes, in her dreams,
she'd feel a flutter in her womb
and then her spirit beamed.

And then she'd wake to truth so stark
and barrenness inside.
The emptiness she felt in life
she truly could not hide.

A decade passed since vows they took,
and still, no babe to hold.
She prayed and pondered on God's oath
to Abe and Sara old.

Their longing never went away,
"We'll strive to trust like them,
and patiently await God's will,
oh please, a child do send!"

The hardest time of all was when
the manger and the child,
appeared to brighten the dark days,
yet on her, more grief piled.

So many times, she'd see the babe,
His tiny arms outspread,
seeming to ask to be picked up,
to hold Him and be fed.

The bed with hay did not bring joy,
it looked more like a cross.
She wept each year the bitter tears
and wallowed in her loss.

The sun marked seasons and then years
and hope began to rust.
Their hearts like rocks so heavy placed
down on grey lifeless dust.

Then came the Christmas of despair,
and dimly, she did pray.
So weak and tired of holding on,
she let go and did lay

her pain down at His feet and said,
"Dear Lord, I give to you,
this worn-out dream I've carried long
and clutched so tightly to."

With burden gone and nothing there,
a space for God to fill
was opened up that holy day,
and in her love was sealed.

She looked upon the child in straw,
His arms outstretched as norm,
but what she saw seemed so different;
it brought peace to her storm.

Instead of begging to be held
Another view she saw –
My arms reach out to save you, dear!
To you, I give my all!

And though she's had no labor pains,
accomplished are her dreams.
For Christ the babe flutters within
and from her soul, He beams.

Note: Cherished family and friends were the inspiration behind "Dreams."
I lovingly dedicate this poem to them and all who deal with infertility.

Leaves Outside a Window

A sky full of
gold-once-green
awaits His command.
Silently being.
Silently trusting.
Silently still.

One in a million
does a dance.
Spinning and teetering
with the joy
of life.

Then it happens;
the leap of faith,
a blissful free-fall.
Silently being.
Silently trusting.
Silently still
    on the ground.

Buried at Attention

Tall timbers,
a ghostly grey
stand close at attention
like the stoic soldiers
that warmed each other
in formation
that cold December day.

Rusty colored leaves
smother the ground
like blotches of blood
that flowed from the bodies
and smeared the earth
that cold December day.

A Mourning Dove soars in,
perching upon the wailing trees
that pleaded for final relief
on that cold December day.

The seasons shift,
the years march on,
and the hardwoods continue their stance
though they don't comprehend
that they have been commissioned
to represent the warriors
who were never buried at attention
that cold December day.

Note: "Buried at Attention" is about a wooded area near where soldiers fought in the Battle of Fredericksburg on December 13, 1862, and a young soldier who tried to help the numerous dying men.

Forgive Them

What hurt more, my Lord?
The striking blows of your captors' fist
while you were blindfolded,
or the striking blows
of Judas and Peter denying you?

What hurt more?
Hearing the leather whip scream through the air
repeatedly slicing open your back,
or hearing the crowd scream
to release Barabbas instead of you?

What hurt more?
Having your skull pierced
with terribly long thorns,
or having the soldiers ridicule and pierce you
with their terrible words, "Hail, King of the Jews?"

What hurt more?
Falling onto the rocky road
with the heavy cross pinning you down,
or the crowd falling in line along the road
to look down and sneer at you?

What hurt more?
Nails being pounded
into your hands and feet,
or the pounding of your disciple's feet
as they ran away and abandoned you?

What hurt more?
Bearing the mockery of others as they jeered at you
to come down from the cross and save yourself,
or bearing the massive weight of the sins of the
whole world while staying on the cross to save us?

Jesus responded to all these hurts,
which include the hurts inflicted by our sins,
with the merciful words he spoke from the cross
before dying for us.

**Father, forgive them,
for they know not what they do.**

Illumined

Bound to the ground
surrounded by dark
loyally attempting
to stay on mark.

My spots of sin
I claim them all
and try to arise
each time I fall.

Longing for mercy,
longing for light –
what's that illumined
above my sight?

Sweet love in flight!
So radiant and free!
Oh how I wish . . .
I wish that were me!

There's a scarlet of hope
and a verdant hue.
I must keep my eyes,
my eyes on you.

Surrender and trust
and obedient glee
I empty myself;
Oh please fill me!

Could it be true?
This motley mess?
Graces bestowed
on me? Why yes!

For you're fully divine
and fully human,
by your sacrifice
I'm free and
        illumined!

Note: "Illumined" is an ekphrastic poem that I submitted for the 2020 Sacred Poetry Contest sponsored by Catholic Literary Arts (https://www.catholicliteraryarts.org/poetry-contest). An ekphrastic poem is one that is written in response to a work of art. The artwork was *Nature and Grace*, painted by Jean C. Wetta (http://www.jeancarrutherswetta.com/Nlandscapes.htm).

Marching Orders

Ring loud the song of truth!
To a world stuck in shrill lies.
Persevere in honest peace,
even if they still deny.

Resound harmonic hope
to those who groan of doom.
With joy sing out your faith!
Though doubt may largely loom.

Make forgiveness a chorus echo,
and break the chains of hate.
And charitably lavish love
on those who acetate.

This is our marching song,
a melody so sweet.
So, Christian soldiers stand.
Let Him direct your feet.

Trust

Hanging by one leg
from a dusty picnic table;
the spider trusts.

Buried in the ground
under dry hard dirt;
the seed trusts.

Waking in the morn
full of hunger in a nest;
the bird trusts.

Sitting on a stool
before a wheel of clay;
the potter trusts.

Holding pen in hand
before empty white sheets;
the author trusts.

III.

Rejoicing

Piney Praise

Thank you for the rain.
For my friends were ablaze,
my cousins were engulfed.

Thank you for the rain.
My sapwood was parched,
my bark was brittle.

Thank you for the rain.
My cones are clean,
my needles are supple.

Thank you for the rain.
My cambium is growing,
my heartwood is full.

Thank you for the rain.
I shine and stretch,
my body is refreshed.

Thank you for the rain.
I dance with the wind,
and sing your praise.

Thank you for the rain.

Note: In September of 2011, Texas was in the middle of a drought. The dry conditions fueled a series of wildfires across the state, with the most devastating in Bastrop County. The Lost Pines ecosystem at Bastrop State Park was part of the devastation of this most destructive wildfire in state history. The inspiration for "Piney Praise" was a 2011 rainstorm in another dry area, the Big Thicket's piney woods in east Texas.

Talking Feet

My feet talk to me.
They do that a lot now that I am getting older.
They chatter about Grand Canyon hikes,
jumping volleyball spikes, and games of tag.

The phalanges yak about hopscotch,
sprinting around the bases, and mountain climbing.
The tarsals and metatarsals recall
when life was strong and fast and free.
Each and every movement-memory
is carefully filed away between the bones.

My timeworn feet rejoice
when God puts a spring in their step,
and a giddy-up in their gallop.
They sing when I waltz with my husband
and they giggle when sand settles in their toes.
My feet celebrate their maker.

My feet also recount the feet of a man who walked
on a rocky road to a place known as "The Skull."
It was a bloody death march,
made by Christ out of love for us all.

His holy feet were punctured with nails
onto the wood of the cross.
They bore the intense weight of all our iniquities.
Not only did he talk the talk,
but he walked The Walk.
And though the path is painful,
I choose to follow His feet.

Birther-of-All

When the treetops are glowing
    and the temperature drops

When the forest grows grey
    and the river turns dark

When the bees go back to their hive
    and bluebirds settle in their nest

When armadillos start rooting
    and possums wake and stretch

When the owls focus their eyes
    and the cool rich smell of a delightful day
    is fading away

My soul soars and says,
"Thank you, Birther-of-All."

In My Own Words

Abba,
you make your presence known
throughout all of creation.
All that lives and breathes
gives praise to your name.

You unite your family
when we follow your path.
Fill our soul and body
with your nourishing grace.

May we reach out with a loving hand
to others who have wounded us,
and we beseech you
to show mercy upon our failings.

Infuse your loving light
deep within our core,
especially when darkness knocks.

All the works of your hands
jump for joy at your majesty.
Truly, my life is yours.

Note: "In My Own Words" developed out of a spiritual activity to write the "Our Father"
in my own words.

Emerald Treasure

Snuggled between
two turn-of-the-century houses
with a family of thirteen in one
and a blind widow in the other,
it stood.

From a seed
at one point in time
to a fledgling sprout in another,
it grew up
and down
at the same time.

By the time
I came to know the tree,
it was mature
and bearing
many, many,
sweet, tart, crunchy, crispy,
green ovals.

My arm stretches,
my toes point,
my hand clamps
and twists.
Snap!

And the tree surrenders
her gift of
an emerald treasure
to me.

St. Philip Neri –
The Joy of Rome

Why is my heart
so poor he prayed,
I want to love like you!
A ball of fire
was the response
and in his chest, it grew.

The ribs did bend
the bones did crack,
so swollen was his chest.
An orb of love
was placed inside
and filled his core with zest.

The joy that flowed
poured out upon
all those whom he did pass.
His piety
and playfulness
drew poor and rich high class.

His cheerfulness
and wit were yes,
the things that lured them in.
Yet love and mercy
for their sins
was what their souls did win.

To those with crimes
too much to bear
he hugged them to his chest,
and then a gift
of warmth and peace
his heart to them did bless.

Can love expand?
Why yes indeed!
With prayer, and grace, and grit.
The Joy of Rome
spread Christ to all
and in their hearts, he lit.

Note: St. Philip Neri is known as the Second Apostle of Rome (after St. Peter) and as The Joy of Rome because of his cheerfulness. He had an incredible gift for love, which he received on the eve of Pentecost in 1544. He was deep in prayer when he saw a ball of fire enter through his mouth and plant in his heart. This intense divine love expanded his heart and caused his ribs to break. Whenever he undertook spiritual practices, his heart would palpitate, and when he had an inconsolable penitent during confession, he found that they were consoled after they laid their head over his heart.

A Visit

A star-cup leaf
dropped in for a visit.
We smiled and said hello.
I told my companion;
You are a hat for my nose,
fitting perfectly on the bend.
You are a good friend,
listening attentively to my whims.
You are a messenger from above,
Full of red glowing light
You are a fallen star,
Please give me your sight.

A wasp
flew in for a visit.
We smiled and said hello . . .

A Pond Psalm

I sing along with the starlings and sparrows,
for his love endures forever.

I spring into life amid the capering cottontails,
for his love endures forever.

I radiate gloriously among the pink peonies,
for his love endures forever.

My heart's aflutter with the chatter of chipmunks,
for his love endures forever.

I soak in the peace of the pea-green pond,
for his love endures forever.

I give thanks to the Lord, for he is good.
His love endures forever.

Note: "A Pond Psalm" was inspired by Psalm 136 as well as the beauty of a Michigan family member's backyard pond and all that lives around the water source.

IV.

Abiding

Breath

I am
but a breath,
an exhale of Love,
a divine puff of wind
that animates
my soul.

Stained Eyes

It's a most distressing disguise
with mossy matted hair
and crusty pleated skin.

It's a most distressing disguise
with grimy tattered robe
and back and ribs so thin.

It's a most distressing disguise
with rusty crooked cart
and wretched hill of heap.

It's a most distressing disguise
with aching famished thirst
and no place to rest and sleep.

Yes, it's a most distressing disguise
that our sweet Savior wears.
It's a most distressing disguise
for which no one seems to care.

It's hard to see through
the disguise of poor and pain
and see The God in all
with eyes so badly stained.

Note: The inspiration behind "Stained Eyes" came from a homeless person who dwells by a covered bus stop on my drive to work, as well as the tireless care that Mother Theresa gave to the poor in the slums. She said to seek "the face of God in everything, everyone, all the time," especially in the poor.

A Trinity Cinquain

Creator
Master Artist
making, molding, bestowing
source of all life
Father

Christ
Incarnate Word
teaching, shepherding, feeding
healer of wounded souls
Savior

Spirit
Holy Ghost
comforting, inspiring, helping
giver of fruitful gifts
Counselor

Trinity
Three In-One
loving, forgiving, renewing
sovereign of the universe
GOD

Love's Embrace

His fingers glide across my face (wind)
His voice whispers in my ears (rustling leaves)
His strong arms hold me up (creek-bank roots)
He smells like sand and cypress

My God and I
in love's embrace

Advent Longing

Many rush through weeks of celebrations
towards the birth of our Savior King.

Some look with expectant contemplation
for his splendid second coming.

I long with hopeful anticipation
for a very personal thing.

My loved ones in reconciliation,
oh, then how my spirit will sing!

Chisos Basin by Night

The reflecting eyes
of the grey fox
point out the entrance
to the dark bowl.

Our steps are slow
on the holy path,
and keenly
we enter the sacred circle.

The icy air
gusts its mid-night
welcome to us.

Ancient mountains,
silent and immense,
frame us
and the tapestry overhead.

Our eyes shoot up
like rockets
at the glittering
diamonds and dewdrops.

We stand like statues,
mesmerized
by the lights of love
piercing holes
into the blackened
canvas.

The tick-tock of chronos ends,
and kairos grace
infiltrates our soul.

A fallen star
streaks,
like cupid's arrow,
across the sky.

And with mouths agape,
the universe of your love
fills the chalice
of our existence.

Note: The Chisos Mountain Basin in Big Bend National Park was the inspiration for this stargazing poem.

You

You formed me.
You used your holy hands to shape me
into the perfectly beautiful child
you always wanted.

You took that divinely created shape of me
and did a most passionate thing . . .
You exhaled your life into me
and I became your beloved.

You beheld me – and I gazed upon you –
as spellbound lovers.

Time has passed,
and I've looked away.
Our unity
disordered by distractions.

Yet when I focus,
I remember your breath
and it sends tingles down my spine.
Just like the first day.
The first day we became one.
That day when your intense, eternal love
created me.

I long
to spend eternity with you.
Help me find my way
back to You.

About the Author

Rose of Sharon is a wife, mother, grandmother, and
elementary school teacher who is passionate about sharing
the light of Christ's love with others via the written word.
She loves the Author of Life and all that He created,
and the beauty of the world flows naturally from her works.

Residing in Northwest Houston, Rose of Sharon
and her husband are catechists for the sacraments of
First Communion, First Reconciliation, and Holy Matrimony.
They enjoy spending time outside, praying together, and
visiting their four grown children and their five grandchildren.

Rose of Sharon blogs at Light of Love, (https://lightoflove.blog/)
and you can also find her on the web at **roseofsharon.net**.